Advance Praise

"I was a coaching client of Karl's fc already learned everything that he . *Chaos* managed to surprise and enlighten me. Many business books make the claim that they'll tell you the 'things that you wish you'd known years ago,' but Karl's new book goes one better: it tells you the things that you need to know, but might not like hearing, in a way that is still palatable and easy to digest. It's eminently readable, even if it's full of hard truths."

—**Chris Dreyer**, CEO, Rankings.io

"Agency leaders are always holding 'growth' up as the ultimate goal, not realizing that the inevitable changes that come with growth are a) less doing and b) more managing. If you have accepted that charge, and still want to grow, Karl's book will help you not hate your life but love the influence you can have on your team. Not a single client will remember your agency two decades from now, but every single team member will remember your management style and the impact it had on their life."

—**David C. Baker**, Practice Lead, Advisory Services, Punctuation

"Karl was an instrumental part of our success here at Pact—he provided critical frameworks to evaluate and manage talent. Most meaningfully, unlike most consultants, Karl rolls up his sleeves and gets down to business with leaders to help solve their trickiest problems. Having clear, actionable advice like this in a book will certainly be an invaluable guide."

—**Allegra Poschmann**, CEO, Pact

"All agencies are born in chaos, and some die in chaos. Karl offers a lifeline for agency owners seeking shelter from the storm. Consider this required reading, and then read it more than once."

—**Chris Bolton**, Founder, Grow Your Agency

"Managing the people in a marketing agency isn't for the faint of heart. In this book, Karl Sakas (my former agency coach) lays out leadership and management advice that his clients, like myself, have paid thousands of dollars to receive over the years. This advice will transform how you manage and lead your team and, most importantly, improve your life and happiness. I guarantee you'll achieve positive results if you implement even a few of his recommendations, such as structured one-on-one meetings, ARCI matrices, or hiring a strong #2."

—**Mike Belasco**, exited agency owner

"Successful growth is tied to how well a founder can pivot to becoming a people leader. It isn't always a natural change, but it's crucial to scaling (and keeping) a team. Karl does a great job breaking this down in a conversational tone."

—**Jonathan Baker**, Practice Lead M&A, Punctuation

"*Calm the Chaos is* the definitive leadership guide that agency owners have been waiting for. Karl Sakas masterfully breaks down the complex challenges of agency leadership into clear, actionable frameworks that deliver immediate results. His unique blend of strategic insight and practical wisdom—drawn from advising hundreds of agencies worldwide—shines through on every page. This isn't just theory; it's battle-tested advice that works in the trenches of agency life. From building strong leadership teams to creating scalable processes, Karl shows agency leaders exactly how to transform chaos into clarity. If you're serious about building a better agency while becoming a stronger leader, this book is your roadmap to success."

—**Chris DuBois**, Agency Coach, Dynamic Agency OS

"Of Karl's extensive work, no book hits closer to my heart than *Calm the Chaos*. I've spent the past decade trying to dispel the false belief that 'agency life' must be synonymous with 'chaos.' Karl has informed my thinking over that time, and now he has armed this rebel with an incredibly practical manifesto."

—**Gray MacKenzie**, Founder, ZenPilot

"Annoyingly, Karl Sakas has done it again—he's created a must-read guide for anyone seeking to transform their agency from a whirling chaos into a well-oiled machine. *Calm the Chaos* delivers the kind of practical, actionable insights that leaders normally shell out thousands to obtain. From establishing a coaching culture and fine-tuning communication with ARCI matrices, to hiring that indispensable #2 and implementing one-on-one meetings that actually work, Karl shows you how to prevent burnout, improve team morale, and get projects running smoothly. Packed with proven tools and grounded in real-world agency experience, this book is your go-to roadmap for sustainable growth, happier clients, and a thriving team. In other words, *Calm the Chaos* is exactly what you've been looking for—just don't blame me when you can't put it down."

–**Carl Smith**, Champion of Humanity in Leadership, The Bureau

For bonus resources to help *Calm the Chaos* at your agency, please visit **CalmTheChaos.xyz**

Calm the Chaos

10 Ways to Run a Better Agency

Karl Sakas

Sakas & Company

Foreword by Gini Dietrich

Ready to accelerate your progress?

Get free resources at CalmTheChaos.xyz

Please send your questions, comments, and feedback (even the typos!) to Karl@SakasAndCompany.com

(FAQ: It's pronounced "say-kiss.")

First Edition

ISBN: Paperback: 979-8-9871445-1-0
            Hardcover: 979-8-9871445-4-1
            eBook: 979-8-9871445-7-2
            Audiobook: 979-8-9871445-6-5

Obligatory Disclaimer:

Applying this U.S. and agency-centric advice will likely help you, but your mileage may vary. I'm not an accountant, lawyer, financial planner, or medical expert. Be sure to get custom-to-you advice from the appropriate professional.

Even if you don't run an agency or other marketing organization, the advice likely applies, too. After all, you want to do work you're proud of, with clients (or stakeholders) and team members you like, while getting paid a reasonable (or maybe *more* than reasonable) amount.

Dedication

Thanks to everyone who's helped me become a better leader, to then pay it forward.

A special thank you to both of my parents (U.S. Army, Retired), who taught me early that leaders eat last.

And to my long-time coach, Laura Westman. As she's noted, life isn't about *doing* all the time; it's OK to just *be*.

Table of Contents

Calm the Chaos

Foreword by Gini Dietrich

When I started my agency, I naively believed that being good at communications meant I would be good at running an agency.

Like many of us in the industry, I was an accidental agency owner—skilled at media relations, content creation, and client service but completely unprepared for the complexities of leading a team.

I had come from a role where I learned exactly what not to do from a leadership perspective—but I hadn't yet realized that the behavior was wrong. Because of my experience, I simply thought that's how you behaved when you were a boss, and I emulated what I had learned.

Then I had a year in business that was so bad, I'm often surprised I kept going. Three things happened:

1. Clients were constantly upset at the level (or lack) of service they were receiving from my team, and I, in turn, would throw bombs into their inboxes late at night after spending all day listening to complaints;

2. My team complained about being burned out, which didn't make sense to me since no one worked more than 40 hours a week; and

3. I had a mean business coach who held no punches. (He wasn't really mean; he was great at his job—I was highly sensitive and prone to lots of tears.)

I will never, ever forget the day that I complained to the aforementioned business coach about my team's inability to do their jobs and how "burned out" they were. I was frustrated, overwhelmed, and completely at odds with their behavior. He let me vent, then said, "And whose fault do you think this is?"

You can imagine how well that went over. It never occurred to me that I was the problem. I thought I was just really bad at hiring. It turns out I had the exact right team; they had the exact wrong leader.

I had to rewire my behavior and change my mindset. I needed to learn how to be a leader.

This is why Karl Sakas' *Calm the Chaos* is such a crucial addition to an agency owner's repertoire. Drawing from his work with hundreds of agencies across six continents, Karl has created more than just another business book—he's crafted a practical framework for the unique challenges of agency leadership.

Karl recognizes that agency leaders must simultaneously be visionaries and operators, creatives and businesspeople, mentors and managers. We face unique challenges in transitioning from doer to leader, maintaining quality while scaling operations, and the perpetual tension between client demands and team well-being. This book provides clear, actionable solutions to these persistent challenges.

Whether you're a seasoned agency leader or just beginning your journey, you'll find valuable insights in these pages. For those just starting out, this book will help you avoid the painful lessons many of us learned through trial and error. For experienced leaders, it offers fresh perspectives and new approaches to persistent challenges. And for those somewhere in between, it provides a roadmap for navigating the next phase of your agency's growth.

In an industry that often celebrates the chaos of creativity, Karl shows us that calm, intentional leadership isn't just possible—it's essential for building sustainable agencies that truly serve both clients and team members. This isn't just theory; it's practical wisdom that works in the real world of agency leadership.

As you read this book, you'll find yourself wishing, as I did, that you'd had access to these insights earlier in your journey. But more importantly, you'll finish it equipped with the tools and confidence to lead your agency forward. In an industry constantly evolving, that's perhaps the most valuable gift any book can offer.

–Gini Dietrich
CEO + Founder, Arment Dietrich + Spin Sucks
Creator of the PESO Model®

Preface

Running an agency will never be easy—but it doesn't have to be so hard. I've helped hundreds of firms break through growing pains, increase their revenue, and scale more seamlessly.

With the right approach, agency owners can work less and earn more—increasing profits while eliminating the need to work nights and weekends.

From running and consulting with agencies over the past two decades, I've learned about becoming a better leader; building empowered and productive teams; and giving back control of leaders' lives without sacrificing their business success. I've shared that wisdom in articles, speaking engagements, and two of my previous books: *Made to Lead* and *Work Less, Earn More*.

But for many agency leaders, that all might sound great–but also impossible. They can't think strategically about how to grow their business sustainably, long term, because there's just too much going on. Putting out one fire after another, lurching from crisis to crisis, just trying to survive while total burnout creeps closer and closer.

It's too common. I can help.

Many years ago, I was on a coaching call with the founder and CEO of a mid-sized agency. They were clearly really stressed. I asked them what they needed from the call, and they said they needed next steps but were too overwhelmed to even know where to start.

We worked through triaging their situation—including team, client, and sales problems. After validating their stress, I shared advice to help enlist their assistant and their #2 for support, recommended next steps to make a difficult decision, and brainstormed how to get fewer interruptions from their broader team.

At the end of the call, I asked how they were doing. They replied that **I had helped them "calm the chaos."** They felt better thanks to concrete tips, new perspective, and a clear path forward.

That made my entire week. And years later, it's still something I help agency leaders do every day.

That's why I wrote this book for you, to make agency life less frustrating and more rewarding. You're busy, so the book is short. You might read it in a couple hours and then refer back to key points. You can also get bonus resources at CalmTheChaos.xyz.

If you're frustrated with aspects of your agency, this book is for you. Although *Calm the Chaos* focuses on independent agency leaders, there is much here that can be useful for in-house agencies, corporate marketing departments, agencies at holding companies, and other work situations.

So let's take a deep breath. I'm serious, do it right now—take a deep breath in and then out. Feel free to repeat.

Now, it's time to shift from being the fire fighter to the fire marshal. **We can put out those fires—and keep them out for good.**

Regards,

Karl Sakas
Agency Advisor, Sakas & Company
Hillsborough, North Carolina

Introduction

You don't have to start from scratch.

Life is easier when you focus on what's most important. But when you run an agency, that's easier said than done. As a client observed, "It's hard to think about what to make for dinner if you have a knife stuck in your leg.

The solution? If you follow 10 key practices most of the time, you'll likely eliminate 80% of the chaos.

The 10 ways to run a better agency

1. Take care of yourself so you can better support others.
2. Accept that you're no longer the sole 'doer' or 'answer person' at your agency.
3. Create the work environment you wish you'd had.
4. Train and coach your team early so you don't have to do their job later.
5. Tell your team what you need from them.
6. Delegate intentionally, not recklessly.
7. Give team members a chance, but not forever.
8. Build a team of strong leaders to support you.
9. Hire a great #2 and a reliable assistant.
10. Create better meetings for yourself and others.

In the pages that follow, I elaborate on each of these practices—including tips to help you implement each one.

But first, let's get on the same page about what I mean by "chaos." And what's a "leader" versus a "manager"?

You get to define what "chaos" means for you and your agency

I'm using the term "chaos" in a relative sense. If your situation *feels* like chaos, it *is* chaos.

For some agency leaders, it's chaotic when a client is a few days past-due on their payment. For others, things aren't fully chaotic until they realize they need to do a significant layoff.

Running an agency isn't the same as trying to survive a real-world war zone. But your stress and frustration are still valid, and it's worth finding solutions. This book can help.

Leader versus manager: What's the difference?

People sometimes ask me about the difference between a "leader" versus a "manager." Labels matter, but not as much as you think.

You may have heard the phrase, "Managers ensure people do things right. Leaders ensure people do the right things."

Consider how it might work at a large corporation: The leaders are the people at the very top of an organization (in the boardroom and the corner office) while managers work in cubicles, overseeing day-to-day operations.

In that model, leaders are in a glamorous strategic role, while managers are prodding their employees to submit their timesheets.

Given the intimate nature of agencies, the "leader versus manager" distinction can get fuzzy.

- The owners are usually actively involved in running the business, whether that's leading teams, doing sales, fulfilling client strategy work, or even sending invoices.
- Someone with an executive title might lead a team, but they might also still take out the trash.
- A team lead, or even an individual contributor, might serve as an informal manager in their area of expertise.

Balance leadership and management

Ideally, you'll *balance* leadership and management. If you're great at inspiration but struggle at follow-through, your team will become disillusioned. If you're great at planning and tasks but don't inspire your team, they'll burn out.

- **Good managers** think like leaders: sharing their vision with the team to reduce or eliminate micromanagement. A little inspiration goes a long way.
- **Good leaders** think like managers: choosing strategies that are workable in the real world. Inspiration is important, but "will this actually work?" is, too.

For our practical purposes, you can treat "leader" and "manager" as relatively interchangeable... because you need both to succeed.

Prioritize what matters most

As a leader or manager, there are endless things you *could* do all day. That can feel overwhelming when the hours in the day are *not* endless.

Fortunately, some activities have a higher ROI than others. Those activities make work easier, giving you room to handle the rest.

In this book, I've distilled those possibilities into an agency leader's top 10 priorities. They'll help you finally stop rushing from crisis to crisis and learn to be proactive, delegate, and communicate in ways that actually work.

If you insist on people coming to you for approval on every decision, recognize that your agency will struggle to grow beyond about 10 people. If you want or need to grow beyond that, the advice in this book can help. (Plus therapy, too, if there are broader considerations.)

Let's dig-in on the 10 practices, starting by putting on your own oxygen mask first.

1. Take care of yourself so you can better support others.

Put on your own oxygen mask first.

It started as a routine Friday morning. I'd had a long week and was looking forward to a light meeting day. Little did I know as I launched Zoom, I was logging into an intervention.

My core team members said they needed to talk about something difficult. They were concerned I was heading toward burnout, or maybe was already there.

They were right. It had been a tough year, both in the business and in my personal life. I'd been pushing myself too hard, and my team had noticed.

I took the intervention to heart. I shifted my approach and things got better. There are still occasional speed bumps, but I've created new structures to make things easier. Many of those changes appear as tips throughout this book.

Likewise, you can't take care of a team if you aren't taking care of yourself first.

Review your daily schedule

During my consulting intake process, I ask new clients a lot of questions. Three are about their day-to-day schedule: What do they *like* doing, what do they *hate* doing, and what do they *tolerate* doing?

If you're doing things you love, the day tends to fly by—in a good way. If you're doing things you hate, every day is hell. And if it's mostly things you tolerate, you likely aren't bouncing out of bed every morning.

As a leader, you have more control over your schedule than an individual contributor. This can be stressful (because people keep trying to add themselves to your schedule) but also powerful (because you can push back if you don't want a particular meeting).

Some random person wants to meet with you? You're not obligated to say yes. You—or your assistant (see chapter 9)—can reply:

> "Thanks for your interest but that's not a match for our current priorities."

Thanks to internal business rules plus hands-on experience, my team knows the meetings I want, and what I don't want. They can schedule and reschedule on my behalf, without having to ask every time. It's great!

How to do a calendar review

Doing a calendar review is one of your most powerful tools as a leader. You look at your upcoming calendar—this week, future weeks, or even several months in advance. And you decide what needs to happen versus what could shift.

Open your calendar for the coming week. Ask yourself:

- What meetings do you like? What meetings do you dread? What meetings are so-so?
- Are there any meetings that happen out of momentum, where you could attend them less often or skip them entirely?

- Based on how your team has evolved, can you shift some of the meetings to someone else? Are there meetings that you can assign someone else to lead, where you now merely attend them?
- Are you having low-value meetings with people outside the agency? Should you cancel some of them now? Should you preemptively decline meetings like those in the future?

I recommend repeating this process each week to see which meetings you can eliminate in the future. I also do a monthly calendar review to see what's coming up.

If you organize your tasks primarily via a task manager or PM software (rather than a calendar), look there. If you primarily use paper, save the paper for a week or two so you can review everything together.

Taking action: 'Heads down' holds and realistic buffers

What if you see that your schedule is full of things you don't want or need to do? Start by talking to your team. How can you give them what they need without their interrupting you?

If you keep getting interrupted by your team, create blocks of time for them to ask urgent questions (I call these internal Office Hours) and then answer the rest on your own schedule. If they need urgent feedback, they should give you a heads up ASAP. And if you're the *only* person who can sign off on certain things, that may be a sign that you need to hire someone or train a current team member to take over.

You can add "heads down" holds to your schedule to focus on activities that require your concentration. I like to add buffers before and after meetings and before and after travel, since I know things will inevitably pop up.

You can use a calendar hold during non-travel weeks, too. Pre-reserve time if you know you'll need to work on sales proposals, create a client strategy billable, coach a new hire, or share feedback on the team's time-sensitive deliverable.

My coaching clients typically pre-schedule months or even an entire year in advance. What about meeting with new clients? My team puts two-hour holds on my calendar for TBD client meetings. We might not know which future client will go there but we've reserved the spot.

If you have absolutely no space in your schedule, you'll want to enlist your team to help you sort this out. At some point you may need to mass-cancel meetings to regroup. That's disruptive but you can't support others without taking care of yourself first.

I share more tips on meetings in chapter 10, and more advice on how to get things off your plate in *Work Less, Earn More*—including the "Do, Drop, Delegate, or Defer" shortcut.

Consider *energy* management, too

You're excited to do some things and you dread others. If you dread a topic, you might drag your feet. That throws off your schedule and you're less motivated for the rest of the day. But you've probably also noticed that you're better at certain *times* of the day and the week.

Find what works for you. You've been working long enough to know when you work best—and when you don't. Are you scheduling yourself accordingly?

A client told me they love morning meetings, because that's when their brain is fresh. That same week, another client said they prefer not to meet until 11 a.m. onward.

Some clients designate certain days of the week as meeting-free days. Friday is most popular. In contrast, I'm OK doing meetings on Friday mornings but tend to do fewer on Mondays. Recognize that meeting-free days mean you'll likely have more meetings on other days.

If you need a lot of heads down time, you might need to reserve half days or *entire* days to do deeper work. Don't try to shoehorn your best creativity into 30 minutes after a meeting with an exhausting client.

Disable most of your alerts

During calls with prospective clients, I'll often hear their computer and phone alerts going off throughout the meeting. The more clients and team members they manage, the more alerts they get.

If you're feeling overwhelmed by alerts, you can choose to adopt a more intentional way of working. Long-term, you'll need to delegate clients to others and add a management layer so that fewer people report to you. But there are steps you can take immediately to reduce the distraction.

I've disabled all of my audible alerts, with just three exceptions: audible alarms on my phone, vibrating alerts on my phone when I receive an incoming call, and vibrating alarms on my smart watch that I set the day before. The result? I don't see an alert or incoming message until I choose to check for it. I still check throughout the day but it's on my schedule, not what someone else wants from me.

Try disabling some or all of your alerts. Plan to check messages on a cadence you choose (e.g., two or three times a day, potentially as a block of time reserved on your calendar). Let your team know how to reach you if it's an emergency. And then enjoy longer stretches of productive time.

Your team *wants* you to take breaks

In my coaching work, agency owners sometimes worry that their team doesn't think the boss is working hard enough—or won't like if the owner goes part-time.

A few years ago, a client said they wanted to move to a new city and use that as an excuse to cut their weekly workload. They didn't want to tell the team they were moving, because they were worried their employees would think the boss was lazy.

I observed that their concern was less about the move and more about redefining their leadership role at the agency. And hiding the move was unwise, because the team would figure it out—and wonder what else the owner wasn't telling them.

Instead, I recommended they talk with the team about how this would create new professional growth opportunities as people took on more responsibilities. If you go part-time, you're probably going to promote at least one of your employees to handle things.

Change can be scary, but it often helps people grow in their careers. When I help agency leaders create and implement succession plans, their team is usually excited to step up. Your stepping away creates new career paths, which makes people more likely to stay longer at your agency.

Stepping away frees your team to succeed

If you prefer urgency, your team is likely used to your pushing to get things done quickly. You might not even be telling them work quickly—but they know you want things ASAP. You may even need to explicitly say if something can wait.

If so, your being away for a day or a week or a month means your team can work without interruption, and take a break from knowing you're going to pop up with a wild new idea. Your team might even be *more* productive when you're away.

This is also why I recommend agency leaders go on an "idea quarantine" after conferences or retreats. That is, wait at least a week or two before sharing new ideas with your entire team. You can share with your #2 or your assistant (see chapter 9), as long as you frame it as "I'm sharing so you're aware, not because I expect you to start implementing this right now."

What if you prefer a less urgent approach that's more go-with-the-flow? Tell the team where they can make decisions on your behalf. When you come back, you'll likely find they made a bunch of choices you'd avoided or delayed. The agency can now move forward instead of being stuck in neutral.

It's OK to do nothing

We all need downtime. It's part of why people think of some of their best ideas in the shower.

Capitalism says we need to be productive. That's not always a good thing. But it's hard to sustain your productivity when you're *only* focused on getting things done. Humans aren't AI; we need breaks to rest and recharge.

When's the last time you took a vacation? The last time you took a vacation *without* your computer? A vacation when you were truly unplugged? As I mention above, your team likely *wants* you to take breaks.

You can rest between vacations, too. When the weather is nice, I'll take a workday break on my screened porch—watering plants, watching the birds, and observing what's happening in the neighborhood. We all benefit from a mental reset.

And if things are just so packed that you *can't* do nothing? That's probably when you need do nothing even more. But don't be too hard on yourself; I know you're doing the best you can at the moment. Ask your team for help; they likely have some ideas and will be glad you asked. For more on that, see chapters 8 and 9.

Get perspective

Late in the year, a client lamented that they were only going to grow two to three percent annually, compared to their 20 percent goal. I acknowledged their disappointment, but noted that most agencies had struggled that year. Some had done layoffs and others had even closed their doors.

They were below their projection but ahead of most other agencies. In the end, they rallied their team and grew 17 percent. But even if they had stayed at two to three percent growth, they'd have outperformed the market.

It's valuable to hear viewpoints other than our own. That's why I have my own coach, even as I help my clients—we all benefit from an outside perspective.

Who's the right person to give you perspective? It might be a mentor, a former boss, a coach, a therapist, a romantic partner, a friend, or even one of your current subordinates.

When you're stuck on a big decision, consider your ideal outcome, versus minimum-acceptable outcome, versus worst-case scenario

Whenever I'm struggling to make a big decision—or I'm helping a client who's similarly stuck—I'll ask a simple yet powerful question:

> "What's your *ideal* outcome? What's your *minimum-acceptable* outcome? And what's the *worst-case* scenario you want to avoid?"

The goal is to define parameters that narrow your decision. You aren't trying to decide everything about your business.

For instance, say you're weighing whether (and how) to fire a toxic client that hasn't paid their latest invoice.

- Your ideal outcome might be to part ways with the client while getting paid for 100 percent of your previously completed work.
- Your minimum-acceptable outcome might be to break off the relationship with the agreement that they won't badmouth you to others, and you'll forgive the small amount they still owe you.
- Your worst-case scenario might be having to keep working with the client because any attempt at terminating the relationship could lead them to refuse payment *and* badmouth you publicly.

In that example, I might recommend negotiating with the client to try to secure the ideal outcome while also working with your lawyer to draft a non-disparagement agreement, where client agrees not to speak ill of you in exchange for your forgiving the past-due invoice.

If you didn't care what they said, you might push harder. And if you really needed the money, you might tread more lightly.

Try this decision framework with your team, too. You can use it to make almost any business decision—and some personal decisions, too. Speaking of personal decisions...

If you're experiencing a crisis, reduce your expectations

As humans, we can only handle so much. If you're in the midst of a crisis situation—divorce, death in the family, health problems, or another extreme situation—don't try to act like it's business as usual.

You don't need to share all the details with your team, but let them know you need help. This is a time when you don't even need to give directions. You can say:

> "I'm currently overwhelmed and I don't even know where to start."

This includes being sick. If you have a migraine during an internal meeting, you don't have to keep going. If you push yourself to do things you wouldn't expect your team to do, you're not being a good role model for them.

It's OK to delegate temporarily during personal or business crises

Delegation can be temporary, too. A client who was in the midst of divorce was enormously distracted, but didn't step away from the business. Their business partner and broader team wanted to help, but the boss was reluctant to relinquish control and let their team step up.

Unfortunately, this created a leadership vacuum—where things needed to happen but no one was doing them because the founder wouldn't let go. See chapter 6 for more on preventing leadership vacuums.

The solution? Having a series of conversations about what they could and couldn't do in that season of their life. And defining what they'd temporarily delegate to their team to handle while they didn't have the time or emotional bandwidth.

The outcome? Everyone was less frustrated, once they accepted reality. The business has since stabilized—and the owner finalized their divorce, to move on in their personal life. The agency is growing again.

Consider if you need to take a leave of absence

What's worse than being 100 percent away from the business? Being there physically but not 100 percent emotionally.

If you're going through an impossible personal situation, consider whether you need to fully step away from the business for several weeks, months, or longer.

After an agency owner's spouse died unexpectedly, the owner took a leave of absence—initially for three months, but extended to six months. In our previous work together, I'd identified gaps in their team and their delegation. The owner filled the gaps and now the team stepped up to help during the crisis.

Eventually, the owner returned to work part-time. Because they made themselves more optional, they don't have to rush to decide what to do next.

The specifics will depend on your situation and the nature of the crisis—including your team size and composition, your personal financial situation, and whether you have business partners. But keep in mind that your team likely *wants* to help, if you ask. *Ask*.

For more on delegation, see chapters 2, 5, 8, and 9.

You're responsible for yourself

Crisis or not, you can and should enlist your team to help. But you're ultimately responsible for yourself. That includes how you spend your time, where you accept or decline meetings, and how you define what work you will and won't do.

As a business leader, you're in a unique spot. Unlike front-line employees, you have a lot of autonomy over what you do on a daily, weekly, and annual basis. If you aren't happy with your work life, you can change it.

Shift your schedule and responsibilities to do the things you like. Don't have someone who can help take on your old work? Make a plan to hire someone else. Can't afford to hire an employee? A contractor might be an option. Can't hire anyone and your current team doesn't have bandwidth? Weigh if you need to stop doing that activity until you have someone to help.

When I start working with new coaching clients, I ask:

> "Think about your agency three years in the future. What's different, and what's the same?"

Then I help them take action to make it happen, including where they can enlist their team to help.

Now that you've put yourself first, let's focus on your team. Onward!

Calm the Chaos

2. Accept that you're no longer the sole 'doer' or 'answer person' at your agency.

Your job is to get results through others.

My German teacher liked to say, "If you want it done right, do it yourself."

To an extent, that's true—but always DIYing doesn't scale. (My teacher was also the long-time president of her HOA, so she apparently had a high tolerance for thankless work.)

As the saying goes: "If you want to go fast, go alone; if you want to go far, go together." How far do *you* want to go?

Consider your personal and business goals. If you're reading this, you're likely in a leadership role at a marketing, creative, or technical agency. You might be the owner, an executive, a manager, or a future manager.

Think about humanity's greatest accomplishments—things like delivering clean drinking water, curing polio, or reaching the Moon. Few came down to the individual actions of just one person. Even when someone is praised as the inventor or creator, they usually led a team. Success is rarely a solo project.

My parents both retired as career Army officers. There's a long-running joke about a group of new officers struggling to put up a flagpole. The solution is for the young Lieutenant to stop trying, and to instead give a single command:

> "Sergeant, put up this flagpole. Let me know if you need any additional resources. I'll be back later."

I don't blame you for trying to put up the flagpole yourself

After all, that's a big part of how you got into a leadership position—as an above-average individual contributor. You're really good at getting things done on your own.

When a client mentions to me that one of their team members is struggling to keep up, they'll sometimes point out: "But *I* can do account management *and* project management *and* client strategy *and* everything else."

Yes, that might be true, but that above-average ability is part of why the agency owner chose to start a business, rather than staying as an employee at their previous firm.

Don't discount your individual-contributor expertise, because that helps you monitor work completed by others. But the doing is largely not your job any more.

Running an agency requires a different skillset. You need to know enough about the day-to-day work to know it's being done to your standard. But your job is to be thinking strategically about where the world needs flagpoles, not installing each one yourself.

What if you *really* want to focus on installing flagpoles?

You have three options if you're a creative or marketing leader who doesn't like managing people:

1. **Accept that your agency won't grow beyond a certain size.** Typically, that's 5-10 people, if you need to continue as the "answer person." If you prefer to run an agency that primarily funds your lifestyle—rather than an agency you want to sell—you're likely all set.
2. **Pivot to a "super consultant" role.** Instead of leading an agency, you'll be a high-fee fractional expert who serves a smaller set of clients as an independent contractor. This requires ongoing marketing and sales efforts to keep your pipeline full. But you won't be managing a team (beyond, perhaps, one virtual assistant).
3. **Become a non-managerial employee for someone else.** If you don't like managing people, you don't *have* to be the boss. You can choose to step away from your agency to become an individual contributor again. You may not even have to close the firm; you could do an acqui-hire sale, where you become an employee at the acquiring firm.

If I haven't scared you away—you want to become a better leader and manager, but you're not sure where to start—you're in the right spot.

You need Desire, Competence, and Capacity from yourself and your team

Being a good leader and manager starts with *wanting* to lead and manage.

At independent agencies, that's not automatic—especially if someone started as an "accidental" business owner, or they've been promoted to leadership from a creative or technical background.

When you or a team member aren't accomplishing what you need, it's usually because you—or they—are missing at least one of the following three things.

When you evaluate an employee, think of a 3-ring Venn diagram that I call **Desire, Competence, and Capacity**:

- **Desire** is *wanting* to do the job. If someone doesn't want to be a leader or manager, they'll approach things reluctantly. It's hard to assess this during hiring, so you have to look for proxies. For instance, if all of their past jobs have been as a graphic designer, do they volunteer a good explanation for why they suddenly want to become a project manager?
- **Competence** is knowing *how* to do the job. If that's missing, people tend to do the job poorly. It's important for you to have a clear definition of what competence looks like so you can fairly assess their skill level. They'll also need training and coaching.
- **Capacity** is having *time* to do the job. Otherwise, things will never fit into the schedule. Capacity is often the biggest gap for leaders—where you have the desire and competence, but not the time.

You need all three to get things done. If things aren't getting done—by you or others—dig into which of the three might be missing. Once you fix that, you'll likely fix the problem.

Insist on New Rope and don't tolerate Wet Twine

It's hard to reach big growth goals without an exceptional team. And it's nearly *impossible* if you have a bad team.

In my coaching work, I use the "New Rope to Wet Twine" scale to consider the quality of your team members. The idea comes from Billy Kraig, via my mentor Stan Phelps.

- **New Rope:** This is the positive end of the scale—the strong, reliable, smart employees who drive your agency forward. They make your life easier and help you grow the agency. They're easy to work with, and they get results. You promote them quickly, and some may eventually start their own agencies.

- **Wet Twine:** This is the negative end of the scale—the employees who make your life harder. They require an enormous amount of your oversight relative to the mediocre quality they produce. And if someone is always creating drama, they're definitely Wet Twine.
- **In the Middle:** These team members aren't quite Wet Twine but they're also not New Rope. You and your leadership team should help develop them into New Rope... or replace them.

In my coaching work, I ask new clients to complete a Team Census. It's an annotated list of every employee and key contractor at the agency, including their current billables, morale, management workload, and whether each person is New Rope or Wet Twine.

Consider your team. Is everyone the New Rope you need? If not, you likely won't hit your growth goals. If you're worried about firing someone, see chapter 1 on tips on making difficult decisions and chapter 7 for termination advice.

Clarify responsibilities via an ARCI matrix

Tired of doing work that someone else should have done? Tired of drama over who did or didn't do their job? I have a solution! It's called the ARCI (or RACI) Matrix: Who's accountable, responsible, consulted, and informed?

You can use this tool to clearly define roles in any work activity, whether it's a major responsibility or a specific task. That way, everyone is clear on their role(s).

To create an ARCI matrix, consider the four key roles for each project, task, or client relationship:

- **Accountable:** Who gets the credit or blame? In the flagpole example, the lieutenant is accountable for it happening. If it doesn't happen or is done poorly, they aren't allowed to blame their subordinate.
- **Responsible:** Who is the person doing the task? In the flagpole example, the sergeant is responsible.

- **Consulted:** Who needs to provide input on the task prior to it being completed? This can take the form of insights, expertise, or additional data needed to get the job done.
- **Informed:** Who needs to be kept in the loop? This may be someone who wants to be updated throughout the process, but often an informed person just needs to know that the task has been completed.

You'll likely put that information into a spreadsheet or other table, so you can see who needs to do what and when. I share more in the *Work Less, Earn More* book.

An agency example of ARCI

Let's say you're the agency owner. After your team built a website, you personally upsold the client on doing a marketing retainer. This includes creating the client's new integrated marketing strategy.

You don't want to do all the work yourself but you want to be sure everyone contributes appropriately. ARCI will help you assign things to the team. For example:

- **Accountable:** As the owner, you're accountable for the work happening. This includes ensuring the team knows the scope, budget, and deadlines.
- **Responsible:** Your strategist is responsible for creating the strategy, to include presenting it the client. (At some agencies, a creative director might handle this.)
- **Consulted:** The strategist will consult with the account manager (to ensure they're following the client's expectations), the project manager (to ensure they're staying within the budget and scope), and a graphic designer (to get copies of relevant visual assets). They might also consult with you (from your wearing a sales hat) to confirm what you promised.
- **Informed:** The PM will let the accounting department know when it's time to bill the client for the final installment.

If you're the agency owner, you are technically accountable for anything at the company—and you'll likely be consulted at key points.

But that doesn't mean you're hands-on responsible for implementing the work.

When you embrace using the ARCI matrix, your team is less confused about who's handling what. And you make it easier to take work off your plate. This creates growth opportunities for your team, including potential promotions and bonuses.

Assign work to the Cheapest Available Competent Person (CACP)

As an agency project manager, I learned to assign work to what I now call the "Cheapest Available Competent Person."

Rather than the best person, it was the best person available right now who fit the budget.

- If I had two equally competent team members who could do the job, I'd assign it to a more junior person because they were cheaper.
- Or if a salaried team member wasn't available, I might assign something to a freelancer. The freelancer cost us more per hour, but in this case they were the CACP at the time.

Of course, don't *tell* someone that they're the CACP. No one wants to be seen as the cheap option. And sometimes it's better to pay more or wait to get the best person, if the work requires a higher level of expertise.

Solicit (and act on!) feedback from your team

Have you asked your team what they need to succeed? Your answer might be different from theirs, so getting perspective can help. After all, your job is to get results through your team.

This doesn't mean you need to act on *everything* you hear. But odds are good that some of your team's suggestions are straightforward and/or free to implement.

It's wise to acknowledge feedback, and explain why you're not doing something people requested. Otherwise, you'll find that people stop sharing feedback.

Encourage 'intelligent disobedience'

In training service dogs, there's a concept called "intelligent disobedience." When the owner wants to do something but the dog recognizes it is unsafe (for instance, crossing a street as a car approaches), the dog refuses to comply.

This works at agencies, too. Encourage your team to push back when you have a bad idea (or a so-so idea that's misaligned to your overall goals).

My team does this all the time. For instance, I'll share an idea I'm weighing and ask what concerns they have. They usually call out things I haven't considered. Sometimes I reverse course; other times, I continue exploring it, but now more carefully.

Intelligent disobedience can require retraining with newer team members, especially if they've been punished for speaking up at past jobs. Earlier in my career, a marketing director took me aside and said, "Karl, just because you're helping row the ship doesn't mean you get to steer." I have since recovered.

Remember how you *wished* you could speak up back when you were an employee? Good news: Being the boss means you get to create the work environment you wish you'd had before.

3. Create the work environment you wish you'd had.

You're the boss; create the right culture for your business or team!

As the boss, you're under a lot of pressure. Your team looks to you for vision, decisions, and answers. You're a role model, whether you want that or not. You might not enjoy that pressure, but you're in a unique spot.

Good news: As the boss, you get to create the work environment you *wish* you'd had in the past. You're in charge now; you can avoid the mistakes of past bad bosses. And within reason, you can choose to defend your team from dysfunctional situations outside your organization.

That's pretty cool—but it also requires being intentional. Otherwise, you'll end up with things you *didn't* choose, situations that unfolded accidentally or because you created a leadership vacuum.

Let's look at how to be intentional, especially through the company culture you seek to create and perpetuate.

Warmth and Competence

According to authors of *The Human Brand*, Chris Malone and Susan Fiske, humans tend toward either toward Warmth (making people feel special) or Competence (focusing on results).

My natural tendency is toward Competence—getting the job done. This might be your tendency, too. Without a dose of self-awareness, Competence is good for short-term results, but not for long-term morale.

In contrast, your focus might be on creating a fun, nurturing work environment. A tendency for Warmth is great for morale, but not always conducive to getting the desired business results.

Ideally, you'll find an approach that's high in Warmth *and* Competence. That is, you lead a team that gets results while generally enjoying working together. Start by committing to both Warmth and Competence, and seek help from your team and your advisors to fill in the gaps. For more on that, see chapter 8.

Authority versus autonomy

A former boss said you should never ask software developers what they want, because they'd only complain and never be happy. That's... one way to look at it.

They took a fairly authoritarian approach to management. That worked to a degree, but it wasn't especially inspirational. At one point, my boss volunteered that after their employees left for a new job, they would likely never speak with them again. And that was largely true.

They were a brilliant problem solver but they didn't like leading others. That was a problem, since they were the agency's Chief Technology Officer. Last I saw, they've gone solo in the super consultant role I mentioned in chapter 2.

You might prefer to let people figure out *everything* on their own. Although the opposite of an authoritarian approach, this has its own problems—including creating a leadership vacuum causing people to scramble to fill in the gaps.

Reflect on the right balance for you. And whatever you choose, be consistent.

Facetime versus results

In my 2016 book *Made to Lead*, I noted: "Decide if you're the kind of manager who rewards 'facetime'... or results." Since COVID, most managers are now more open to people working remotely. But for this to go smoothly, you'll need to shift your mindset from prioritizing facetime to focusing on results.

Managing remotely is harder than managing in person. You need to set clear expectations about how you'll measure results, including what "done" looks like.

As a shortcut, enlist your team to help define the standards. If you don't like what they draft, you can always request changes. And if you *do* like what they drafted, congrats—you didn't have to do all the work to figure it out.

I'm still a fan of at least some in-person interaction. If your agency is mostly or fully remote, you would benefit from in-person team retreats at least once a year.

Trust but verify

During the Cold War, U.S. leaders adopted a Russian saying: "Trust, but verify." That is, you'll trust what people say... but you still want to double-check occasionally.

Some of this will be asynchronous, like having salespeople make weekly updates you can review before the sales management meeting.

Here are some other asynchronous "trust but verify" options:

- Go into the PM system to see if they're logging notes on key tasks.
- Review AM call recordings to see how they're handling meetings.
- If a salesperson isn't hitting their quota, check their activities in the CRM. Sales activities don't guarantee revenue... but *no* activities definitely won't produce results.
- Confirm you have a signed contract with the new client before their kickoff meeting.
- Compare hours logged to hours budgeted to see if estimates are accurate.

Other aspects will be synchronous, like asking the status of something in a 1:1 meeting if you have followup questions to understand the details. Or once a month, you might sit-in on the weekly department meetings to take in the "vibe." You could also do monthly skip-level meetings with your direct reports' direct reports to see what people are experiencing with their manager.

You can delegate some of this. For example, your management team can double-check most work by their direct reports. But take time to check the managers' work, too, since bad managers create even bigger problems.

If someone has a strong track record, you can pull back on your review. But there's value in checking here and there, because anyone can slip.

And when it comes to embezzlement, it's *always* the people you trust— because if you didn't trust them, they likely wouldn't have access to your bank accounts. (Tip: Ask your bank to send duplicate statements to your home address, so you can review each month. And make it known that you do this.)

Speed versus accuracy

With enough resources, you can do work quickly and accurately. But on a day-to-day basis, you need to choose: Is this task (or broader project) mostly about speed or about accuracy?

The book *Meltdown* (Clearfield and Tilcsik) warns about the dangers of tight coupling. A complex system is more likely to break if interconnected tasks have minimal buffers between each task. If your flight connection is just 30 minutes, even one problem on your earlier flight means you'll miss the second flight. You might now have to wait hours or potentially even days for the next seat. In contrast, a 3-hour flight connection means your scheduled trip will take longer but it's also more reliable.

Make tight coupling part of your internal conversations. For instance, I sometimes ask my team to rearrange our marketing schedule so we can add something new at the last minute. They'll point out the tight coupling and ask if it's worth the risk. If it is, we'll discuss how to reduce the odds of things breaking. And I accept accountability if things go poorly. See chapter 2 for more on ARCI and intelligent disobedience.

As a leader, you have to decide what qualifies as tight versus loose coupling at your agency. If you choose to prioritize speed, you'll want to add resources to double-check the work. You'll also have to accept the errors that inevitably come with a "move fast and break things" mentality.

If you choose to prioritize accuracy, you'll need to manage expectations about things taking longer than the client might prefer. And you'll also want to build guardrails to ensure that the team doesn't do four or five rounds of QA when one or two would do.

Tolerance for mistakes

Speaking of mistakes, how will you handle errors? *Meltdown* notes that individual mistakes are often systems failures, rather than personal ones. That is, it's hard to avoid mistakes when someone works in a broken system.

It's easy for bosses to say, "It's OK to make mistakes." But saying that is different from actually making it part of your company culture.

What's your tolerance for mistakes? What if someone makes a *pattern* of mistakes? What about the same mistake over and over again? What about a one-time mistake that's catastrophic?

If you choose to tolerate—or even embrace—occasional mistakes, make sure people are taking time to debrief on what happened. Discuss what led to the mistake and how we can prevent it in the future.

Ideally, you'll also publicly celebrate when people self-report mistakes. If you teach people that they won't automatically be in trouble, you're more likely to hear about problems before it's too late to fix them.

Business versus personal

I believe that no business should refer to itself as a "family." You're not a family, bound by blood or kinship; you can fire people if they aren't meeting expectations.

Beyond that caveat, you can choose to operate a more businesslike culture or a more personal culture.

For instance, I worked at an agency that did a happy hour most Friday afternoons, weekend volunteering, and cake for each employee's birthday. I worked at another agency that would host employees at the owner's house once or twice a year, but otherwise employees never met up on a social basis outside of work. The agencies were similar in headcount.

Neither is right or wrong (although I'd personally prefer something in between). The main thing is that when you're the boss, you get to choose.

If you have a social committee, give them guidelines on what is and isn't OK. For instance, you might cover one or two drink tickets per person, rather than an open bar. Or if you *do* have an open bar at an event, make sure alcohol is served by venue employees where their liquor license is on the line.

As a manager, you need to stay arms-length from employees. It's OK to celebrate their personal milestones, but not everyone will want to talk about them. If you have happy hour, join for the first round (and ideally pay for it). After that it's time to leave to let your employees connect without you surveilling the conversation.

Introverted versus extroverted

We can define company culture as the behaviors that are encouraged (or even rewarded) versus those that are discouraged (or even punished).

This tends to include whether you lean toward extroverted or introverted team activities. I worked at an agency that had a policy that if someone said "Good morning" to you, you were explicitly *not* required to respond. This was a particularly introverted policy.

Another past employer provided free lunch every day. But the assumption was that if you accepted the free lunch, you'd eat together in the main conference room and you wouldn't leave the office for "alone time" at lunch. Almost everyone stayed for lunch—it was a nice benefit—but it helped that people got along pretty well.

Experience versus culture fit

You'll see plenty of articles that say, "Hire for culture fit, not experience." That makes for a good meme, but you're ideally hiring for both.

Entry-level hires won't have as much experience, although you can look at work and leadership experience from when they were in school. Culture fit might be all you have to go on for an early-career hire. But be careful not to let that turn into hiring people who are identical to you and current team members. This leads to groupthink and can hurt your long-term growth.

Do you need to hire people who have prior agency experience? It depends on the role. If they'll be client-facing, understand how their past stakeholders compared to your clients. If someone hasn't worked at an agency before, dig into their expectations—including why they want to switch to agency life, with its many pros and cons.

Being a picky recruiter requires spending time on recruiting, and it also requires a commitment to building your firm's employer brand. If you become an employer of choice (by creating a good work environment for going good work), you'll get better job applicants. More high-quality applicants makes it easier to hire for experience *and* culture fit.

It'll take time, but it's worth it

Your ideal company culture won't happen overnight and it requires ongoing maintenance.

For example, I worked with an agency that typically promoted managers from within. This was good for culture fit, but it also meant employees hadn't worked for managers elsewhere. This perpetuated problems with boundaries, fraternization, and more. We worked to shift their approach, including additional training and coaching around workplace norms. It paid off: revenue and profits are up, and one of the worst department directors is now one of the best.

Change starts by recognizing that you can be your own kind of boss instead of automatically repeating what past managers have done. And then it means finding the balance between stepping in versus letting things unfold naturally.

With consistent effort—plus a little luck—you can be proud of the result. Being proactive helps, too; read on to see why, and how to take action accordingly.

4. Train and coach your team early so you don't have to do their job later.

Support your team proactively.

As the new president of a marketing association chapter, I led 15 people on my executive team, 100 volunteers, and 700 members. I'd never led a 700-person organization before... and now everyone looked to me for direction. I quickly realized why so few members pursued becoming president.

One of my VPs said they didn't have documentation on how they and their team could do their job. I apologized for the lack of documentation and said it was their job to now create it.

In retrospect, that was unfair of me. I should have invested more resources to support the new VP. That would have included insisting that they meet with their predecessor to learn more about the role before they accepted.

Volunteering is one thing; business is another. If your *agency* is missing key documentation and training, you've got to fix that or it's going to cost you money, stress, and time.

Make a list of training and documentation topics

When it comes to training and documentation, it's a lot like risk management. Start by focusing on three areas:

1. What's *most* likely to happen?
2. What might not be as likely to happen, but would be *catastrophic* if it did?
3. What if things go *really* well?

If you don't have much documentation now, ask your team to make a list of what they don't know how to do. The goal is to create an initial list to form the basis of your future prioritized roadmap.

Of course, they won't know what they don't know—so you'll want to get input from other sources, too. This might include speaking with other agency leaders you know; reading my *Work Less, Earn More* book; or joining an agency community where you can ask questions.

Assess what you have and what you need

What's missing? What's there but needs to be updated? What's in good shape but isn't being followed?

You'll want to work with your leadership team—and they'll get input from their direct reports—to see what needs attention. That doesn't mean someone will document every topic immediately, but you want to know where things stand.

Close the training and coaching gaps

Now, triage the list. I recommend prioritizing quick wins (things you can implement and see progress on right away) with longer-term needs (things that will take longer to document but that will make a bigger overall impact).

You'll probably delegate execution to your leadership team. For instance, if you're the CEO, you might assign this to your COO. If you're the COO, you might assign this to your director of operations or your operations manager.

You won't write all the training or do all the coaching yourself. But it's your job to make sure the training exists, that the coaching happens, and that it's working. In my coaching work, I sometimes see agencies that have excellent documentation that people don't follow. In that case, you'll need to determine why.

If you choose *not* to prioritize certain topics that you know people care about, let them know where things fit in the roadmap. That is, you're not ignoring them—but you're choosing to prioritize something else, and you'll get to their priorities at X point in the future.

Hire for good judgment

Have you ever had a team member make a decision that made you wonder, "What were they thinking?!?" If they had sufficient information to make a good decision but still made a bad decision, it's possible they have poor judgment.

When clients mention an employee has poor judgment, I used to try to coach the agency leader on coaching the team member. But nothing seemed to work.

My conclusion since then? As a manager, there are limits on how much you can help a person improve their judgment. They might naturally improve over time. And you can try role-playing exercises and other simulations to accelerate their progress. But there's no overnight shortcut.

How to hire for good judgment? Ask them behavioral interview questions about their decision-making process ("tell me about a time when..."). Also, pay attention to whether your job opening makes sense as the next step in their career.

And create a ramp-up plan for new hires and new promotions.

Create a "ramp-up" plan for new hires, and for internal promotions

When you hire someone new—and when you're promoting an existing team member—set clear expectations about progress.

The ramp-up plan will detail what you expect from them in Week 1, Week 2, Month 1, Month 2, and beyond. Many of my agency clients frame it as a "30-, 60-, 90-day" plan.

What's the key to a successful ramp-up plan? Consider these steps:

1. Identify the role's key performance indicators (KPIs).
2. Choose an escalating set of monthly KPI targets you expect them to hit as they acclimate to the role.
3. Get the new employee's buy-in on the plan and the metrics.
4. Review progress each month and hold the employee responsible if they aren't hitting their ramping-up KPIs (or revise the plan, if you realize that your assumptions were off).
5. Terminate the employee if they continue to fail to meet their KPIs. (More on that in chapter 7.)

Here's a simplified ramp-up for a mid-career account manager:

- **Month 1:** Schedule "get to know you" calls with 90 percent of their assigned clients.
- **Month 2:** Lead 100 percent of their ongoing client meetings.
- **Month 3:** Schedule in-person or video meetings with 90 percent of their assigned clients' bosses, to better understand their business and personal goals.
- **Month 4:** Lead a majority of any client renewals, with their manager shadowing the conversation. Identify opportunities to grow all of their accounts by at least 20 percent this year.
- **Month 5:** Handle 100 percent of client renewals, and pitch 100 percent of clients on the upsells identified last month.
- **Month 6 (and beyond):** Secure client satisfaction ratings of at least 90 percent on each round of client surveys.
- **Month 12 (and beyond):** Grow their account base (total accounts managed, in dollars) by 20 percent year-over-year.

If they're more senior (e.g., an account director managing an AM team), you'll expect higher sales goals plus metrics around their direct reports' performance. If they're more junior (e.g., account coordinator), you'd evaluate activities and client satisfaction rather than retention and upsells.

In contrast, a subject matter expert (SME) hire—like a designer or developer—might focus on increasing their weekly billables. In Month 1, they might be at zero hours/week in billables as they onboard, and then at 32 hours/week by Month 6.

The benefit of a ramp-up plan? You and the team members know if they're on track. If you've never hired this particular role before, you might need to make more adjustments as you go. The key is to approach the process as a two-way conversation rather than an executive dictate.

This also helps you see people who have high potential. On a recent hire, I saw a team member was doing Month 2 work in Week 3. Later, they were supposed to handle 10 percent of a CRM migration but ended up doing 90 percent of the migration. Combined with their other successes, I promoted them early.

The new-hire ramp-up plan is especially important for sales and marketing lead-gen roles, where it's easy for people to make excuses about why they're not hitting their quota. Instead of demanding 100 percent immediately, you might assume zero percent of quota in Month 1, 10 percent in Month 2, 30 percent in Month 3, and growing to 100 percent in (say) Month 8.

Create a coaching culture

I recommend committing to creating a coaching culture at your agency.

What does that mean? You and your managers focus on helping people improve. You ensure people get the support they need, including documentation and other resources to do their job. You let people try to find their own solutions first, but you also don't leave them flailing.

You pre-schedule check-ins if someone's doing a task for the first time, rather than dismissively saying "figure it out." But you also encourage people to stretch, if you see greater potential in them than they see in themselves.

If someone makes a one-time mistake, you work with them to understand what went wrong—and enlist them to solve things themself, if possible. You also look for opportunities to share this lesson-learned with others.

That doesn't necessarily mean you celebrate failure—and you should create guardrails to prevent grievous errors, or repeated errors—but mistakes often create opportunities for everyone to learn and to fix broken parts of your agency's systems.

As Winston Churchill said:

> "Success is not final, failure is not fatal: it is the courage to continue that counts."

Have ongoing 1:1 meetings

Managing people is tough—especially when you're putting out fires. Running your agency is a lot easier when you're proactive, but it's hard to make time to plan ahead.

Fortunately, one small-yet-powerful change can make a *big* impact: having weekly 1:1 meetings with your direct reports.

I do this myself as a manager and my top-performing clients do the same. I follow the agenda format from Manager-Tools.com:

- **Them:** 10 minutes about what the employee wants to discuss
- **You:** 10 minutes about what you want to discuss
- **ProfDev:** 10 minutes about their professional development

That first of the three sections is really important. Why? You're creating space for your employee to ask about whatever is important to them. This also saves them from interrupting you another time.

I open each 1:1 by asking simply: "What would you like to discuss?" This gives them an opportunity to get advice, talk things through, or just share about life in general.

After their first 1:1 with me, an employee in their early 30s said: "That's the first time a boss has ever asked me what I wanted to talk about." If you were an employee, you'd want a boss who listened, right?

The third section is a mix of long-term planning (e.g. discussing leadership opportunities, or up-skilling that requires more than a few hours), and short-term changes (e.g. confirming they made a process change you requested, or that they followed up about a high-priority item).

Just 30 minutes a week per direct report can help you boost employee retention, get work off your plate, and prevent future problems.

Recognize that most people aren't magically ready for their next role

Consider a phased or step-by-step approach to promotions. Let people succeed at earlier roles before you promote them to the top.

When I'm helping clients create internal succession plans, promotions might look something like this: individual contributor, lead, manager, director, VP, and beyond.

Not everyone wants to make each leap, and not everyone can. But if your promising team lead struggles as a director, they're unlikely to succeed as a VP. They also might need longer to get there.

Be careful not to overpromise future promotions. For instance, you might think a strong AM has potential to eventually become the VP of accounts, or even the president with you as CEO. For now, talk with them—and their manager—about a path to account supervisor and perhaps account director. Don't talk about their potential as a VP until they prove they can perform in the interim roles first.

What if you're in a hurry to promote someone fast because you want to get out of the role yourself? That's a dangerous spot. If someone realistically needs two to three years to prove themselves, but you expect them to succeed in six months... it probably won't end well.

Put yourself in their shoes. As my robotics teacher in high school warned, "Be careful if a company offers you a job after just one interview." That is, they're not being careful to ensure you're a fit and that rarely goes well for you *or* them.

Be especially careful if you're promoting (or hiring) someone to become the head of the agency. If they're an external hire, add 18 months to the ramp-up timeline, because you don't know their capabilities *or* their character.

Sometimes people need to leave to get new experience, before they come back. A "boomerang" employee can be an ideal leadership hire if they left because you didn't have opportunities for them several years ago, but now they have what you need. Of course, don't rehire someone if they're a terrible fit; familiarity isn't the only factor.

Adjust when you see more (or less) potential than an employee sees in themself

Sometimes people aren't confident in their own potential. As a leader, you may have experienced some imposter syndrome yourself.

Part of your role is to help people reach their potential. Not everyone wants to do that—or will successfully achieve that. But you can certainly try.

The flip side? When someone is overconfident. Be honest about your assessment of their competence and help them improve. But you have to talk to them. As much as you might wish it were the case, they can't read your mind.

5. Tell your team what you need from them.

Your team can't read your mind.

A new team member started at my company on Monday. By Thursday, I observed that they seemed to be reading my mind. I asked how they did it. Turns out, they'd once supported nine executives at once. In comparison, supporting one business owner was easy.

I've been lucky in hiring several people who can read my mind. (Or as a friend snarkily observed, half of the mind-reading might be that I'm predictable.)

Most leaders aren't so lucky. Instead, you need to be clear about what you expect—what success looks like and the guidelines to follow.

Give your team a clear vision to follow

Several years ago, I reviewed a client's employee engagement survey results. There was a troubling pattern—the owner had a clear vision for their future, but the team didn't know it.

They were asking relatively basic questions, including:

- What's our long-term revenue goal? How fast do you want us to get there?
- Are we going to add new services or stick with the current ones?

- Will there be opportunities for us to grow as the agency grows?
- Are we going to stay at this office, move to something bigger, or go remote?

Most of that was clear in the agency owner's head—these were things we'd discussed in our coaching calls—but they hadn't shared it with their team.

I recommended a new goal: Share answers to these questions during the upcoming all-hands meeting, and work on making people feel safe enough to ask other questions they might have held back.

After the all-hands, I asked how things had gone. Several employees told their managers they were relieved to have the answers. One didn't like the growth goal, saying it seemed unrealistic. But now their manager (and the owner) understood the source of the resistance and could engage in a productive conversation about it.

Make it easier: Values, Goals, and Resources

Make sure your team knows the Values, Goals, and Resources (VGR) you want them to keep in mind.

I created the VGR framework after noticing my agency clients kept getting questions from their team about what to do. More than one client has told me they're tired of getting interrupted all day long.

Want fewer interruptions? Make sure the entire team knows the VGR to follow at your agency and for each client:

- **Values:** What activities are rewarded versus discouraged? Are there boundaries no one should cross?
- **Goals:** What should your team accomplish? What does success look like?
- **Resources:** What resources are available to complete the work? This includes time, money, people, software, and knowledge repositories.

Taken to the positive extreme, VGR enables you to reduce your interruptions and empower your team. You might eventually say:

> "As long as you follow the VGRs, I'll support whatever you do. Sometimes, I may ask you to do things differently in the future, if I realize there's a new VGR in play. But you won't have to redo your previous work."

And if you don't trust someone to follow the VGR? It's probably a sign they aren't a long-term match.

Set clear expectations

As a manager and leader, your job is to share the Values, Goals, and Resources the team should consider in getting the job done.

This doesn't include telling them exactly *how* to do the job, since you want them to have the freedom to find their own solution (as long as it fits the VGR). If someone has never done something before, it's OK to walk them through your process—as long as you're clear about what's "must do" versus "how I do it."

This includes being clear about what success looks like. For instance, if I delegate something to my team, I might say:

> "I'd like your help launching the new lead magnet. You'll serve as project manager—including coordinating with the designer and scheduling my inputs—and you'll build the relevant components in the CRM. I'm on board with your recommendation to feature the <popular asset>, as the best match for our business goals.
>
> Here's what success looks like. The new lead magnet will be active on the website at <specify> locations, new signups will get the lead magnet, and we'll do a new nurture to introduce them to our free and paid content. This will be active by <date>. We'll review progress a month later, to identify any tweaks.
>
> Please schedule a check-in for us to review progress at the halfway mark. And let me know when I need to provide input

before or after that point. You're also welcome to enlist <designer> and <other team member>.

What questions do you have about what I shared? <pause for Q&A> Please recap your understanding of the assignment. <listen, and tweak if needed>

Thanks! Please proceed, and let me know if you need help prior to our check-in."

Their sharing a recap helps you confirm they understood the assignment. Now's the best time to ensure they're pointed in the right direction.

Use the "3 A's" of communication

The 3 A's are a simple-yet-powerful approach to improving internal agency communication. They are:

- **Aware** — Your employee just wants you to be aware, but they'll handle it.
- **Advise** — Your employee wants your advice, and then they'll proceed.
- **Actively involved** — Your employee needs you to take ownership in solving things.

When someone on your team tells you about a problem, ask them which of the 3 A's they need from you. That is, are they sharing to make you aware, because they need your advice, or because they need you to become actively involved?

Using the 3 A's makes your life easier because you don't automatically have to jump in to fix things—especially when all they wanted was to make you aware or to get your advice.

Likewise, it makes your employees feel better at work because they have the autonomy to solve the problem themselves while still keeping you in the loop. If you tend to get sucked into solving your team's problems, adding this checkpoint can help save you from yourself.

Do debriefs to learn from past experience

I'm a huge fan of debriefs. When I run events, I debrief after each session and after the program as a whole. I ask three questions:

1. What worked?
2. What didn't work?
3. What will we do differently next time?

Debriefs can help you fine-tune your team's activities—and that includes their making better decisions without needing to consult you as often.

Consider how to organize the results of your debrief so that the right people see the results. After all, it doesn't help if new hires or other relevant team members can't take on the institutional knowledge.

If someone *can* read your mind, do your best to retain them

Assuming they're a match in other areas, too—if you discover you have hired a mindreader, keep them!

Calm the Chaos

6. Delegate intentionally, not recklessly.

Practice delegation, not abdication.

As a consultant for marketing and creative agency leaders, it's usually the agency owners themselves who reach out to me for help, or a second-in-command who's been tasked with finding an advisor.

But I sometimes hear from agency employees, who find me on their own, and ask if I can "fix" their boss. Unfortunately, there's not much I can do if their boss thinks they don't have a problem.

In these situations, the boss usually does have a problem. And that problem is what I call a "leadership vacuum—where the leader isn't leading, and the team steps in to do their best.

The problem is that in leadership vacuums, the team is trying their best to do a job they haven't been trained, empowered, *or* authorized to do. Because they're not the owner (and they're often working without the owner's knowledge), this rarely ends well.

The solution? Delegate, don't abdicate. Don't expect your team to always "figure it out" when it's your job to provide guidance.

Let's look at examples of delegation and abdication. Let's say you're about to head out on a two-week vacation, and you normally handle almost all of the sales process yourself.

Here's a comparison between the two:

- **Delegation:** You ask your director of operations to handle sales screening, scoping, and closing. You share expectations, set pricing parameters, and brainstorm potential situations. You pre-schedule time to prepare and then debrief on how it went. You also reassure them you trust their judgment.
- **Abdication:** You leave for a two-week vacation and tell them to figure it out. Or worse, leave without saying *anything* and they have to guess what to do while you're away.

Delegation is harder than it looks

Has someone ever told you to "just delegate more"? That doesn't help! You already know you're supposed to—but it's hard to actually do it.

Part of the challenge is that "delegate more" actually involves 15 or more steps—and over 20 steps if you need to hire someone new.

The 15 steps for good delegation

1. Recognize that you can't (or shouldn't) do the task yourself.
2. Consider what portions of the task to delegate so you can hand them to someone else.
3. Identify how you'll later integrate their deliverable(s) into your own workflow, if applicable.
4. Identify the skillset(s) required to define the role(s).
5. Of the current team, identify who's competent to handle this.
6. Confirm that they're available on your timeline, budget, and other specifications.
7. If the right person isn't on the team now, find and hire the person (or people) who can do the work.
   a. Decide whether this should be an employee, an individual contractor, or another firm.
   b. Identify prospective candidates who can do the work.
   c. Interview the candidates to assess their competence.
   d. Make an offer to the finalist.
   e. Negotiate rates—including hourly rate, salary, or project-based fees.
   f. Get them under contract.

8. Decide how you'll communicate tasks to the people who are helping.
9. Transfer knowledge to them about the goals and specs to consider, including sharing access to relevant resources.
10. Pre-schedule a check-in with them at an appropriate time to review their in-progress work before the deadline (especially if this is a new relationship or a new task).
11. Do a mid-way check-in.
12. Share constructive guidance as appropriate.
13. Get the final deliverable.
14. Confirm QA on the deliverable.
15. Integrate the deliverable into your workflow, if needed.

Fortunately, you don't have to do each one of these steps every time. If you have someone on the team who's done the work before, you might just tag them in your PM system and they can take it from there. But the full 15-step delegation process is always lurking in the background.

Delegation is easier when you have shortcuts

Here are some delegation shortcuts:

- **If you have to keep redoing the work:** Are you clear on the definition of success for each thing you delegate? When I assign something, I'll frequently be explicit about that: "The ideal outcome is a v0 rough draft, where I can share feedback for you to create a v1 for us to discuss."
- **If you don't want to make time to delegate:** Your team can't read your mind; you need to explain what you're trying to accomplish. If you don't like writing, share it during a meeting or by recording a screen share video. Then plan on an interim check-in to help them adjust before the deadline.
- **If you have trouble communicating the steps to follow:** Don't focus on the steps—focus on the outcome you want, and on providing the access people need. For instance, you can't say, "figure it out" if they don't have a login to the system.

- **If you're not sure anyone really needs to do the task:** Stop doing it! Manager Tools calls this "delegation to the floor."

These following tips might not always save time, but they can help you overcome delegation-related obstacles:

- **If you don't have someone to do the work:** Weigh whether to hire an employee, a freelancer, or an outside vendor. For instance, a freelancer or outside firm can handle bookkeeping, but ideally client-facing project managers are employees.
- **If you can't afford help:** That's a tough situation. You might temporarily ask a current team member to help with this. Or perhaps a freelancer.
- **If your team isn't competent:** You need to help them become more competent. Assuming they have the potential, this usually involves training them yourself, or pointing them to outside resources.
- **If your clients expect you to do it all yourself:** You can eventually transition client work, once your team has the Desire, Competence, and Capacity. Some clients won't like this; you can offer them their current rate to work with your team, or a higher rate if they want to stick with you. (For further advice on delegating clients, see my book, *Work Less, Earn More*.)
- **If you still don't trust others to do the work:** Ask yourself whether this is about competence—it might be—or something deeper that's specific to you. If your team is competent and trustworthy, you might need to work through this with your therapist.
- **If you don't have time to delegate the work:** Delegation always takes more time the first time, but then you start seeing significant efficiencies. Imagine the time you'll have saved by the 20th or 100th time someone else did what you used to do.
- **If you like doing certain things yourself:** That's fine; keep doing them. But be clear with yourself that this tradeoff may cause problems elsewhere.

Decide between inclusive and exclusive delegation

Depending on your comfort level—personally, and with the person you're delegating to—there are two ways to delegate.

- **Inclusive delegation:** If a topic is on a list you provide, they can handle it on your behalf. If it's not on the list, they need to ask first.
- **Exclusive delegation:** Unless the topic is on the list you provide, they can handle anything else without asking.

If someone is newer to your team, consider the "inclusive delegation" approach (where they have a growing list of what they're authorized to do). In contrast, a long-time team member (where you know their skills, judgment, and character) might have a longer leash.

I recently advised a client on defining guardrails for a trusted employee. I recommended an exclusive approach—as long as the COO wasn't selling the company or agreeing to a contract over a certain dollar amount, they could take appropriate action without asking first. Of course, they'll still talk with the CEO, but the COO can take action without bugging their boss every time.

See chapter 9 for more on working with a #2 specifically.

The better you delegate, the more optional you can become

If you want to sell your agency, acquirers tend to prioritize your EBITDA history—that is, your trend of profit margins. But beyond earnings, they also consider how soon you can step away. You can think of it as making yourself increasingly optional, by delegating key roles to your team.

When you're more optional, an acquirer can feel confident about paying you more money up front and letting you step away from the business sooner (for instance, leaving in 1-2 years instead of 2-3 years).

Even if you never want to sell the agency, being optional means you can do the work you like, instead of the work that you *have* to do. That's great for your peace of mind—and it creates opportunities to grow your team, as they take on things you no longer do yourself.

For more on making yourself optional, see (yes) my book *Work Less, Earn More*.

7. Give team members a chance, but not forever.

Your agency isn't a charity.

You aren't providing lifetime employment to your team. If someone isn't doing their job, they don't get to stay forever.

This happens to be one of several reasons why *not* to hire family members. But this chapter applies to non-relatives, too.

Be clear about your expectations

If someone doesn't have a current job description, it makes it harder for you to claim they aren't doing their job. Sure, most employment is "at will." But team members deserve a chance to perform.

If you've let things slide before, you need to speak up now. For example, you might say:

> "In the past, we've ignored XYZ. Going forward, we have new expectations. <Elaborate on the changes> Are you committed to meeting those expectations?"

If you find that a particular team member needs far more explanation than others, they might not be in the right role.

Coach your team on coaching their team

As your agency grows, you'll add new layers of hierarchy. You won't manage everyone yourself anymore—which has pros and cons.

On the positive side, you likely have several people reporting to you, and they manage the rest. This means fewer interruptions because your managers have handled most issues before problems get to you.

On the negative side, it means you may not hear about problems soon enough. And it means you will need to get good at coaching your managers on coaching their team.

This is a great opportunity to use the Socratic method: "What do you think you should do?" When a manager brings you a problem, ask what options they're considering. This helps you understand their thought process. Ask about the alternatives they're considering. Ask what might happen if they choose each option.

Resist jumping in to personally save the day. For a reminder on using the 3 A's of communications (Aware, Advise, and Actively Involved), see chapter 5.

Part of being a leader and manager is letting your team solve most of their own problems. Your job is to talk before and after they take action. This includes sharing the VGRs to consider as they take action.

Beware the 'good at their job, but...' team members

Several of my agency clients have had team members who were good at their job but who didn't like being on a team or dealing with coworkers.

I call this the "misanthropic loner." That is, they prefer to work solo and resent being on a team. Unfortunately for them, agencies aren't solo organizations: they're team-based, with high role interdependence.

Do not tolerate anyone who's good at their job but problematic in other ways—like the salesperson who exceeds their sales quota but who also harasses coworkers. They need to go.

Escalate your warnings

Most situations merit giving people a chance—or more than one chance—to turn things around.

This usually includes a verbal warning, followed by a written warning, followed by a formal performance improvement plan (PIP).

The PIP gives the team member a short period of time (e.g. 2-6 weeks) to demonstrate new behavior and achieve new results.

If you operate in a geographic location that doesn't require PIPs, they're still a good idea for your employer brand. It's not a good look if an ex-employee can accurately tell former coworkers and the public: "And they didn't even warn me."

As I've said elsewhere, it's easier to let things fester but that rarely helps on a long-term basis. This includes if someone is on the road to getting fired.

Prepare for the termination

Work with others on your team to prepare. That may include your #2, your assistant, and your HR advisor. If things are tense, this will also include your lawyer.

Create a termination packet, outlining the timeline, how to access their benefits, and what needs to remain confidential. Some of this is required by law, like details on health insurance continuation. But beyond that, do what you can to make things go as smoothly as possible.

When you're paying severance, get your lawyer's advice. This may include language about non-disparagement and other clauses to protect you and the agency. It also includes the return of company equipment.

You'll also decide whether the termination is immediate, or if you're giving them notice before a future final day. I've done both. When a contractor wasn't working out, I gave them the option to take up to two weeks to wrap up their current work. They thought about it over the weekend, and said they wanted to end sooner. In less-cordial cases, I coordinated with others on my team to lock out company accounts.

It's never ideal to do the physical or digital version of "marched out of the building by security," but you'll need to choose the approach that fits the circumstances.

Keep it short

Ideally, the termination conversation will last just a few minutes. The individual's manager should do the firing. That's part of the responsibility of being a manager.

If you're in a termination meeting or call longer than five minutes, you've probably messed up. This isn't the time to discuss all the details, and it's not a negotiation.

Get to the point. For example:

> "Unfortunately, I haven't seen the turnaround we need. Today is your last day at <agency name>. You are terminated effective immediately. We are providing X weeks of severance. Our HR lead has just emailed additional resources to your personal account. That includes how to return company property and options to access the health insurance after this month."

Take a break... and then debrief

In my experience, you'll likely feel a mix of emotions.

You might feel relieved that it's over and that you and the agency can move on. But you also might feel guilty about ending someone's current livelihood and self-doubt about whether you could have done things differently.

Even if you could have made better choices before, that doesn't require keeping a poor-fit team member forever.

Take time to rest and recharge. But then, debrief with your team:

- Looking back, were there warning signs before you hired them? What did their references say?
- Was there anything the agency could have done differently? Should you have taken action sooner?
- Is this a sign of broader problems at the agency that you need to address?
- Do you need to take action with anyone else?

Be careful about getting into situations where it feels like an employee is holding you hostage. Everyone is eventually replaceable, even if it will create some short-term pain. At some point, it's time to let the positive uncertainty outweigh the negative certainty.

Are you on the fence about firing someone? I've advised agencies on more than a few terminations. And in my experience, every leader agrees (if not immediately, then eventually) that they did the right thing.

Now, let's look at the roles that help you create a strong team—whether today or over time as you can afford the help.

Calm the Chaos

8. Build a team of strong leaders to support you.

As a leader, you don't go it alone.

In volunteering, the joke is that your first job is to recruit your replacement (because otherwise, the organization will never let you leave).

I'll share more about having a great #2 and a reliable assistant in the next chapter. But really, you need an entire team—working within your agency plus outside supporters.

This also includes succession planning agency-wide. As with volunteer roles, everyone is going to leave the agency eventually—including you, someday.

Embrace your role as a coach

As a leader, your job is to get results through others. Some of that starts with training your team and hiring the right people in the first place. But beyond that, it comes down to coaching.

As a coach, you help your team reach their full potential. For a few employees, that's becoming a member of your executive team, or even your #2. For others, it might be about becoming the best account manager possible. And sometimes, it's concluding they aren't a match.

Coaching is important but it can't "fix" everyone. People need Desire, Competence, and Capacity to succeed. If someone is Wet Twine, coaching will only go so far. And if someone has poor judgment—they have all the info but keep making poor choices—you likely can't fix that.

Don't take it personally if your coaching can't help a team member solve an unsolvable problem.

Don't try to have all the answers.

When I'm facing a difficult challenge, I love asking my team for advice. I benefit because I don't have to think through all the options myself. I also benefit from the team's perspective, which is different from my own.

The team benefits because they're shaping the direction of the company. And they can also see that I respect their experience and opinions.

I don't ask about something if I've already decided, or if it's something where I'm the only one who can decide. But for everything else, it's a win/win when you stop being the sole answer person.

Identify and share career paths for key roles

When I do my culture survey at agencies, client team members often report feeling confident about the company's future, but less confident about their own role at the agency.

When I dig deeper, it's often because people don't see a clear career path at the agency. Sometimes, that's unavoidable; if you have five people, there's limited room for advancement. But if you have 50 or 100 or 1,000 people, there's room for growth.

Career paths include helping people see progression in their role (e.g., from account coordinator to account manager to account director to VP of client services), or the flexibility to shift to a new track (e.g., from project manager to operations manager). But this also necessitates making it clear that promotions aren't guaranteed, and a change in career track is, in part, contingent on business need.

Not everyone wants to—or should—become a manager. As your agency grows, consider opportunities to create technical or SME paths. For instance, someone might move from developer to architect—where they advise on high-end technical challenges but aren't a people manager. You don't have to create a non-manager SME path, but it will certainly help you retain great technical and creative leaders.

Build and run a leadership pipeline

In leading the trade association chapter, I had a secret weapon: a strong leadership pipeline.

For years, leaders would recruit new volunteers and give them opportunities to succeed through a relatively structured process. Someone would start as a committee member, then get promoted to become director of the committee. Eventually, they might become VP of their department, overseeing several directors. Some would choose to pursue another VP role to learn a new area.

Most volunteers left within a couple years but a rare few would work their way up to president.

Of course, not everyone would make it to the top—and not everyone wanted to do that. Some team members were happy to stay as directors for years, as the leader of their specific area. Others got promoted to VP and struggled with the new role... not ideal, but better than jumping from director to president.

You can do the same thing at your firm. Once you define the career paths, think about how to help people move up. This includes clarity on expectations at different levels, along with ongoing discussions about what it'll take to move up.

This doesn't fall solely to you. Set the priority, and then get your executive team's help implementing the leadership pipeline program.

Consider opportunities to give people executive facetime. When one of your directors mentions a high-potential front-line employee, consider doing a 1:1 with the junior team member to learn about their goals and to encourage their growth. A 30-minute meeting might be routine for you, yet career-changing for them.

If someone has potential but there aren't opportunities to promote them, be honest about the situation. Let them decide if they want to wait or go elsewhere. That honesty increases the odds of their coming back in the future, after they (and the agency) have grown.

Ultimately, slower promotion can be a win/win. You see how people perform at earlier levels, and they can decide if they *want* the increased responsibility.

And if they're like my former coworker who expected to become a department director by age 24... they'll probably self-select out of the agency.

Hire externally when you can't promote from within

As engineering manager Kate Heddleston notes, there are two ways to get great people: "make" them or "steal" them.

Ideally, most promotions would be from within—where you know their potential and their character, and where they don't have to learn how the agency works to succeed in their job. Indeed, internal promotions are a good default strategy to put great people into important roles.

However, you won't always have existing employees who'll be a match. Sometimes you need a new skill set or a different level of experience. Or maybe a current team member has potential, but doesn't want the promotion.

In those situations, you'll need to steal someone great by hiring externally. But as you know, external hires can be risky. You don't know if they're a match for your agency or even as competent as they claim to be. As a mentor told me in college, some candidates will say *anything* to get a job.

The solution? A structured hiring process, including a clear job description; a widely-cast net for the recruiting process; a paid assessment to evaluate their skills in job-relevant areas; and rigorous reference checks to ensure you aren't hiring a con artist.

Include your current team in the interview process when you're doing an external hire. They'll likely notice issues that you might miss.

Be careful about promoting someone to their first management job

Managing people is hard. As you've probably experienced in your own management and leadership journey, doing an individual contributor job is very different from managing people who are individual contributors.

I recommend offering training, coaching, and opportunities to take on escalated responsibility over time. Here's what each of those covers:

- **Training** doesn't solve everything, but it gives new managers a vocabulary and a great sense of "knowing what they don't know."
- **Coaching** helps people improve, including custom 1:1 guidance to help them navigate situations that go beyond their training alone.
- **Escalated responsibility** lets people learn and make mistakes in lower-risk settings.

For instance, before you make someone a department head, see how they do as a team lead. This usually means they're advising and coaching junior team members, but the lead isn't a formal manager.

Do check-ins to give you time and structure for coaching. I'm a fan of weekly 1:1 meetings, and you might need to meet more often when someone is new to a role. The idea is that employees need space to ask questions, rather than feel like they're always "interrupting" you. See chapter 4 for more on 1:1 meetings.

During this coaching, go back to the Socratic method—by asking genuinely open-ended questions that lead the employee toward discovering the right answer on their own. Don't extend this forever (at some point, you'll want to give an answer), but this approach can help people reach their own conclusions. And in my experience, those lessons stick better than just telling people what to do.

Think about succession planning across all levels of the agency

Succession planning goes beyond the executive level. Is your agency helping project coordinators become project managers? Are you helping graphic designers become art directors? Otherwise, you risk losing your investment in promising talent—and you'll need to start all over again with someone new.

Coach your leaders on thinking about succession planning within their teams. And consider how you can reward their developing others, since they're making life better for you and everyone at the agency.

Encourage (and pay for) professional development opportunities

When I advise agencies on hiring, I recommend asking candidates what they do for professional development. I'm less concerned about the specific answer, and more concerned that they have *some* answer. Our industry evolves too quickly for people to be static.

Beyond their taking initiative, you want to give employees time and money to support their professional development. This includes a profdev budget, and not requiring them to use PTO or vacation time to go to training.

You can "veto" profdev activities (e.g., they want reimbursement for a certification entirely unrelated to the agency's needs). And people still need to complete their main job.

Don't forget yourself! You're reading this book, which helps. What *else* will you do for professional development this year?

Build an extended team

Beyond your employees and core contractors, consider building an extended team of advisors and support staff.

In my work with agencies, these roles may include:

- Therapist
- Coach(es)
- Lawyer(s)
- HR consultant
- Accountant and/or tax advisor
- Insurance agent
- Financial planner
- Personal trainer (and potentially a nutritionist)
- Spiritual advisor
- M&A advisor (if you plan to exit)

For more on this list, see my *Work Less, Earn More* book.

Now, let's dig deeper on two key roles who'll likely eventually become your closest colleagues at work: your #2 (second-in-command) and your executive assistant (EA).

Calm the Chaos

9. Hire a great #2 and a reliable assistant.

Want it or not, we all need help. Getting help makes you a better leader.

In my experience, every high-performing agency leader has a strong support system. They usually have a formal #2 (second-in-command), often have an assistant, and ideally have both.

Why? As an agency project manager, I saw that it's hard to PM yourself. That is, we lack perspective on ourselves. I'm naturally organized—several clients have called me "the most organized person they've ever met"—but my team helps me stay that way.

The Entrepreneurial Operating System (EOS) refers to personality types they call the Visionary and the Integrator. If you're the Visionary, you need an Integrator—someone to turn your vision into reality.

My model is to consider whether you're a "Starter" or a "Finisher." As a Starter, we benefit from a Finisher who can make things happen. And you're a Finisher, it helps to have a Starter to get things moving.

You can wear multiple hats. As a coach, I help clients translate their vision into goals that their #2 can implement. And as agencies grow, the leader's #2 sometimes has their *own* #2 (the #3, I suppose) to support them.

Imagine building a relationship where you can describe your vision to a colleague, and they make it happen. This requires communication, trust-building, and experience. But I've seen it happen—in my own business, and for my agency clients.

This typically includes selecting and nurturing a second-in-command, and also hiring an assistant to support you on the more granular details. You and your #2 might opt to both work with the same assistant.

Defining your ideal #2

The book *Riding Shotgun: The Role of the COO* (Bennett and Miles) notes that the chief operating officer (COO) role tends to be "bespoke" to each CEO. If the CEO leaves, the COO usually leaves, too (unless they were being trained to succeed the CEO).

Your #2 will likely be a bespoke role, too. Sometimes it happens accidentally—where you create a leadership vacuum and someone unofficially steps in to fill the #2 role. Ideally you realize you need help and ask a current team member to officially become your deputy.

Consider your strengths and weaknesses. What are you trying to accomplish? If you have big growth goals, you might need to hire someone who's helped an agency accomplish those goals before.

Finding your ideal #2

If you don't already have a great #2 in place, you'll need to find them. The ideal #2 has worked at multiple companies, giving them a broader perspective on how things can and should work.

A client's #2 started as an intern and now serves as president. They'd never worked elsewhere, so my coaching gives them perspective on alternative options. Another client is preparing to promote a long-time employee to VP, then president, then CEO. I'll shift my coaching from helping the founder to helping the newly promoted employee as they lead the agency.

If you need to hire externally, take your time. I know you're eager to get someone onboard ASAP, but this is the most important role you'll ever hire. Similar to working with a business partner, you're effectively "business married" to your #2. It's better to have *no* #2 than to hire a *bad* #2. You want to get to know their character, ensure you and they work together well, and confirm they fit with your team. See chapter 8 for more on the "hire externally vs. promote from within" topic.

Consider a ramp-up plan (see chapter 4) for external hires in which they don't immediately start as president or CEO. When I build succession plans for clients, people usually spend at least a year in each stepping-stone role. They can go faster if they hit certain benchmarks. And in some cases, they might need a bit longer—or you and they may conclude that they aren't a match to continue upward, and you'll need to find someone else.

How I found my current #2—and future #2

I met Diane, my current #2, through a marketing trade association. We'd volunteered together for two years before she joined me as an employee.

I particularly appreciated her willingness to speak up when there was a problem, versus the cultural norm of "go along to get along." She initially said she'd stay for 18 months; she's now at nearly seven years. For when she eventually retires, Diane helped me find her future replacement—Kate.

Diane and Kate are individually amazing, and they work together well. I'll miss Diane when she retires, but I know I'm in good hands with Kate.

Kate proved herself early—going above-and-beyond on CRM migration and website launch projects. As she's continued to do well—including taking on managing others—she just received her second promotion.

You never know exactly how things will go. But life is easier when you have a great team.

Working with your ideal #2

Each "#1 and #2" relationship is unique. You need to find an approach that works for you. But I tend to see some common factors. As the #1, consider these points:

- Treat this as your most important business relationship. That includes sharing openly with your #2. That includes respecting their time; other than for an emergency, don't cancel your scheduled check-ins.
- Be clear about what you're trying to accomplish. This usually includes sharing the Values, Goals, and Resources you want them to consider. When you do this—and have the right person on board—you don't have to micromanage them.
- Pay attention to their list of priorities. Although you shouldn't micromanage, it's important to know where they're focusing. Let them know if your priorities have changed.
- Take their advice, and explain if you won't follow it. Your #2 can be a key advisor to you. But that requires generally *following* their advice. If you do something else, explain why. Otherwise, you risk training your #2 to stop sharing advice, which reduces how effectively they can make your life easier.
- Look for ways to develop their career. That includes helping them grow at your agency. Sometimes that means pointing them elsewhere if your agency is no longer a fit.

Parting ways with your #2

Everyone eventually leaves. The ideal #2 manages your expectations and ideally helps you find their successor. They're able to think about the good of the company rather than solely about their personal needs.

Sometimes that means people stepping down because they're not what you need any more.

A past client's #2 had been a loyal team member for years and had become the director of operations. But as the agency grew, roles became more specialized. The #2 wanted to do a different type of work than what the agency needed, yet the agency wasn't big enough to need that new kind of help. It wasn't their fault, but they weren't the right #2 any more.

In my 1:1 interview with the employee, I observed that they were becoming increasingly disgruntled at work. I recommended to the owners that they help the employee find a new job, in the hope that they might return in the future.

Things didn't end well. The two business partners disagreed about what to do. A year after I suggested a graceful transition, they fired the employee after things devolved.

Be proactive, and talk about what you need versus what they want. If you aren't aligned—for instance, you want to triple the size of the agency, and they don't—help them find a new job and hire a new #2. It's not a fun process, but you need to do what's right for everyone involved—including yourself.

Assistant vs. #2: What's the difference?

There's overlap between what your #2 does and what your assistant does, especially for agencies under 10-15 people.

The big difference is their level of autonomy. Your #2 can usually act on your behalf. Your assistant sometimes can act on your behalf, especially if they function as more of a chief of staff.

When you have 10-20 people, your #2 might be a director of client services, a VP, or perhaps an operations manager. They're usually leading an area of the business, but they're also effectively your deputy. As a shortcut, consider: if you're on vacation, who's officially (or unofficially) in charge?

If you're the CEO of an agency with 50 or more people, you'll likely have a COO or president as your #2. (And if you've become 100% optional, you might be the chair of the board, and your CEO is *technically* your #2... although at that point, you're not involved in day-to-day operations.)

Your assistant might have one of these titles: chief of staff, executive assistant (EA), administrative assistant, virtual assistant (VA), or administrative coordinator. At smaller agencies, the operations manager or even a project manager might serve as your assistant as one part of their broader job.

What your assistant does

Regardless of their title, your assistant's job is to help you be as productive as possible. Sometimes this involves saving you from yourself. Other times, it's saving you from others.

For most agency leaders, their assistant helps with scheduling, follow-ups, and travel booking. They may serve as project manager for internal initiatives. They may also serve as your "gatekeeper," especially in blocking external parties from your schedule.

For many of my clients, their assistant joins meetings to handle post-meeting follow-ups. Similar to an account manager or project manager on client-facing calls, your assistant might send the post-call recap and ensure that people do what they are committed to do. When my team joins a call, I love that I can run the call—but not have to personally manage all the follow-ups.

Working with an EA is a two-way street

Respect your assistant. Their job is to assist you, but they aren't your servant. Sometimes you need to get your own coffee—and ask if they'd like some coffee, too.

My approach is to share more rather than less. The more they know about what's going on—including access to my email and my calendar—the more they can help me.

Not everyone gets that close, and you don't need to *start* by delegating email access. But if you're reluctant to share everything, consider whether your unwillingness is about them or you.

You should expect the following from your EA: discretion, gatekeeping, accuracy, decorum, initiative, adaptability, questions, service mindset, judgment, autonomy, candor, industry acumen, tech savvy, firmness, and humor.

But you also owe the following *to* your EA: respect, fair compensation, appreciation, input, clarity, boundaries, backup, and time away from you.

Knowing when to hire a #2 or an EA

Every agency leader (whether an owner or executive) needs an assistant or someone else providing some degree of administrative support. If you can't afford a full-time person yet, that's OK; start with a part-time virtual assistant to start.

As a leader, your job is to focus on what I call your "$1,000 an hour" activities. You might not bill that much for your time (and indeed, you might be trying to minimize your client-billable time), but it's a helpful analogy. "Is this activity the highest-value thing I can do for the company? And if not, should I drop, delegate, or defer it?"

Sometimes clients say, "I'm not sure what I'd have an assistant do for me." When we dig into this, there's always *plenty*. Once you find the right person, you'll keep finding more for them to do. And part of their being the right person means they'll proactively recommend things they can handle for you.

When it comes to hiring a #2, timing can be fuzzier. As a shortcut, consider: 1) do you need someone to manage people who report to you, and 2) do you need to launch major initiatives but don't have the time or expertise?

When I recommend quick wins to new clients, I modulate the recommendations based on what they can accomplish. For instance, a two-owner team with a strong #2 can accomplish a lot more than a solo owner who doesn't have a strong #2.

Knowing when to fire an EA or a #2

If there's insufficient Desire, Competence and/or Capacity, give them an opportunity to turn things around. If they're a good person who's ultimately in the wrong role, consider helping them find a new job. It's the right thing to do, and it'll be better for everyone involved. Don't let things fester.

Your #2 and your assistant require a lot of mutual trust. If they've done something serious to lose your trust, you may need to terminate them. Why? Because there's not really a way for them to regain your trust, and you'll keep wondering what untrustworthy thing they'll do next.

10. Create better meetings for yourself and others.

Meetings are part of your job, so make them better.

I have a 1972 book on running better business meetings. It opens by asking readers:

> "Should you even have a meeting?"

Decades later, companies still struggle with this. But now you're in a position to make things better, one meeting at a time!

Meetings aren't the enemy; *bad* meetings are the enemy

Think about a great recent meeting. You probably felt a sense of accomplishment and even camaraderie. You got things done, and you were glad you met.

Now, think of a not-so-great meeting. It may have been a waste of your time, or you didn't achieve your goals, or everyone left unhappy.

Some meetings are unavoidably difficult—like when you need to give a client bad news. But if we set those aside, your choices drive whether a particular meeting was great versus meh versus terrible.

It's not just the volume of meetings—it's also the *quality* of the meetings. If you commit to better meetings, you can start making life easier for everyone around you.

Do a meeting audit to understand your current commitments

Take a look at the calendars across your agency:

- What are your meeting commitments?
- What about your leadership team? What are their meeting commitments?
- How about your front-line employees? What are they facing?

While reviewing the results of your audit, keep these questions in mind:

- Do you prefer to spread out your meetings or to group them on certain days?
- Could you attend certain meetings weekly instead of daily, or monthly instead of weekly?
- Can some people skip the meeting, sometimes or always?
- Do they all need to be meetings, or would another format do the job?

The exact solutions will depend on the problems you notice. But it all starts by doing the meeting audit to know the situation.

Synchronous versus asynchronous: Finding the "just right" approach

Ideally, live ("synchronous") meetings are only for things that couldn't happen outside a meeting. This includes brainstorming, solving problems or making decisions about complex topics, and connecting with fellow team members to improve working relationships.

Otherwise, ask yourself if this *really* needs to be a synchronous meeting. If not, "asynchronous" can work. For instance, everyone posts an update by a certain deadline, and then people review on their own.

What if people don't have time to read things on their own? Consider a hybrid approach.

Hybrid meeting format: Start with "study hall"

Information designer Edward Tufte recommends an approach he calls "study hall."

Here's how it works. First, print a packet of key materials for people to read and have the packets ready when people arrive for the meeting. Then, spend the beginning of the meeting as "heads down" time for people to read the packet. Finally, discuss questions.

The idea is that if people don't have time to read beforehand, they can read (silently) at the beginning of the meeting. This requires extra prep from you as the organizer, but it can pay off by making meetings better for your entire team.

I did this as president of the marketing trade association chapter. Board members shared updates beforehand in a consolidated dashboard, and then everyone read the updates at the beginning of the meeting.

We didn't waste time with everyone talking endlessly, people got the info they needed, and we had time to do activities like brainstorming and problem-solving that truly are best handled in a live meeting.

Avoid agenda-less meetings

Other than relationship-building meetings, most meetings should have an agenda. What are you trying to accomplish?

If someone asks to meet but doesn't say why, ask them to elaborate. You don't need all the details, but you need the basics. For instance:

> "I'm running into a problem with XYZ client; I've identified two options and wanted to get your feedback on which to use."

That means you need to include details, too. Don't just direct-message someone on your team and say, "Hey, can you meet?" Instead, include some context before you hit send. For instance: "I have some questions about the XYZ report, and wanted to discuss it before you send it to the client. Can we do a video call this afternoon before you send it externally?"

Don't skip the "meeting before the meeting"

It's popular for people to complain about the "meeting before the meeting" or the "meeting after the meeting." But that's short-sighted.

If you're presenting a big deliverable to a client, you'll want to coordinate internally on who's doing what. You might even meet with your day-to-day client contact first, before you present something to their boss.

You'll also want to debrief after big meetings. I debrief after almost every external event: what worked, what didn't work, and what to do differently next time.

If you run from one big meeting to another, it's hard to make time to learn from past meetings. Buffers can help make it easier. If you find you don't "have time" for buffers, that's probably even more of a reason to have them.

Use buffers

A client was a few minutes late for our coaching call. They apologized and said this was their eighth meeting of the day.

That sounded truly miserable. But it gave us a new priority in coaching—how to make their schedule better. In addition to delegating client meetings to their team, we also looked at adding buffers between calls.

You can create buffers in your scheduling software, or add buffers in your calendar. I do both. This has several benefits:

- All of my self-scheduling links pull from the same pool of spots, so I don't have to manually go back and forth—or risk double-booking.
- I create buffers before and after client calls. Depending on the client's track record, they might get a shorter or longer buffer.
- You can limit the number of meetings in a day. If your typical day has 6-8 meetings (or more), it's hard to start (or make progress on) anything else.

Start with short buffers and see how they help. I suspect you'll add more buffers soon. And yes, you can reserve time on your calendar for lunch, therapy appointments, and working out. This includes reserving time to create *and* implement your plans.

Want more scheduling tips? See my advice in chapter 1.

Calm the Chaos

Challenge: Apply what you've learned!

It's time to practice this advice.

It's time for the rubber to meet the road. You've likely started applying tips from the book as you've read along.

Write an Advance Retrospective to visualize your ideal future

It helps to visualize your ideal Calm the Chaos future. In my coaching work (and in my life in general), I created a tool I call the "Advance Retrospective" to help make that happen.

How does it work? Write about your ideal future day. I suggest picking a day that's about five years from now.

Open a new document and start with this sentence:

"Today is <future date>. It's a great day because..."

And then keep writing.

There's no right or wrong length (although my agency clients tend to write 1-3 pages). And you can take your time. People will often write for a bit, set things aside, and come back to add more later.

If you're trying to decide between different future paths, you can write two versions of the Advance Retrospective. Likely, you'll find that one is a lot more fun to write... and that might help you choose the path. For more on making difficult decisions as a leader, see chapter 1.

Want the best results? I recommend that you share a shortened version of your Advance Retrospective with your leadership team. Go ahead and remove personal details but don't keep your ideal plan a secret from people who can help you get there faster.

Create a 30-60-90 day plan to grow

Now, let's be strategic. If you were to outline a 30-60-90 day plan based on what you've read here and noticed about yourself along the way, what would that look like?

Outline that plan now: What will you do in the next 30 days, the next 60 days, and the next 90 days?

Then, enlist a trustworthy team member to help you stay on track. We can't project manage ourselves; we all benefit from support.

Is there more to making this happen? Yes. But a good PM will help you create the structure you need to deal with the rest of the moving parts and help you stay on track.

Bonus: Thank your best past boss

Who was your best leader or manager? If they're still alive today, send them a thank-you message. I bet they'd love to hear that they made a difference.

And if they've since passed—or you can't find them—honor their legacy by being the best leader and manager *you* can be. You've got this.

You can do it!

As we conclude, I hope you're leaving feeling more empowered and inspired. Management and leadership are hard, but they're easier when you commit to improving—and you've already demonstrated commitment by reading this book.

If you've gotten value from this book, please share an online review so that others can experience it for themselves. And if you meet a leader who's struggling, encourage them to get their own copy.

Thanks for reading, and good luck in your leadership journey! I'd love to hear how it goes. Please reach out via the book website at CalmTheChaos.xyz.

–Karl Sakas (karl@sakasandcompany.com)

Calm the Chaos

Additional Reading

There's always more to read. Here are books that may help in your journey as a leader and manager.

Anything You Want (Derek Sivers)

Built to Sell (John Warrillow)

Crucial Conversations (Grenny, McMillan, Switzler, etc.)

The Effective Manager (Mark Horstman)

The E-Myth Revisited (Michael E. Gerber)

The Five Dysfunctions of a Team (Patrick Lencioni)

Founders at Work (Jessica Livingston)

The Goal (Eliyahu M. Goldratt)

How to Win Friends & Influence People (Dale Carnegie)

The HUMAN Brand (Chris Malone & Susan T. Fiske)

The Leader Lab (T. Luna & L. Renninger)

Lost and Founder (Rand Fishkin)

Made to Lead (Karl Sakas)

Managing Humans (Michael Lopp)

Managing (Right) for the First Time (David C. Baker)

Managing to Change the World (A. Green & J. Hauser)

Meltdown (C. Clearfield & A. Tilcsik)

Radical Candor (Kim Scott)

Same as Ever (Morgan Housel)

The Splendid & The Vile (Erik Larson)

Traction (Gino Wickman)

Turn the Ship Around! (L. David Marquet)

Got a favorite book you'd add to the list? Let me know! You can reach me via CalmTheChaos.xyz.

Also by Karl Sakas

Calm the Chaos: 10 Ways to Run a Better Agency (2025)

Work Less, Earn More: How to Escape the Daily Grind of Agency Ownership (2023)

Made to Lead: A Pocket Guide to Managing Marketing & Creative Firms (2016)

The In-Demand Marketing Agency: How to Use Public Speaking to Become an Agency of Choice (2015)

Hundreds of articles since 2013 at SakasAndCompany.com

Calm the Chaos

Acknowledgments

Although it's my name on the cover, this book is very much a team effort. Specifically, thank you to:

- **Barbara Blythe** for early feedback
- **Brayian Zakia** for accountability support
- **Chrissy Stallions** for the cover
- **Claire Busic** for content marketing support
- **Diane Stadlen** as a sounding board and more
- **Eli Webb** as sound engineer at Sonark
- **Gini Dietrich** for writing the foreword
- **Jen Becker** for intellectual property guidance
- **Jenna Routenberg** as copyeditor
- **Kate St. Cyr** as project manager and sounding board
- **Melissa Breau** as marketing strategist
- **Mike Belasco** for advance feedback
- **Nicole Capó Martínez** as content strategist
- **Noémi Zillmann** for eBook conversion
- **Paul Panfalone** for the chapter illustrations

Thanks to everyone who shared an "advance review" blurb—and to my clients, past and present.

Finally, thanks to you as the reader. If you like the book, please tell one person about it—and then share an online review to help others benefit, too.

Calm the Chaos

About the Author

Karl Sakas helps marketing leaders Work Less and Earn More, while rewarding their best team members. He is a fourth-generation business owner.

As a management consultant and executive coach, Karl has personally advised hundreds of agency owners on every inhabited continent. Through his team at Sakas & Company, Karl offers coaching, consulting, and training.

Channeling his background in agency operations, his clients often call him their "agency therapist." Karl has written four books and hundreds of articles on agency growth. Outside of work, Karl volunteers as a bartender on an antique train.

Want to keep growing? Get additional resources here:

- SakasAndCompany.com
- CalmTheChaos.xyz
- WorkLessEarnMoreBook.com
- AgencyTherapy.com

Printed in Great Britain
by Amazon

60155488R00060